ACKNOWLEDGM.

First is a thank you to my wife Maria or as I call her, Pea. Why? Because we go together like peas and carrots, so she is my Pea. She is a person who is so understanding and dedicated to me and our family and for allowing me the opportunity to take time away from her, and our children, and grandchildren, to write this book or anything else that is needed to benefit our family. She is my best friend, my soulmate, my rib that truly protects my heart. She works with me, and puts up with me daily at my office. I want to give a big shout-out thank you to her.

Regulatory Issues

This publication contains the opinions and ideas of its author. The strategies outlined in this book may not be suitable for every individual and are not guaranteed or warranted to produce any particular results. The author is not an attorney, and does not give legal advice. Presentations of performance data herein does not imply that similar results will be achieved in the future. Any such data are provided merely for illustrative and discussion purposes rather than focusing on the time periods used or the results derived. The reader shall focus instead on the underlying principles.

these ideas after determining if they are appropriate and suitable for your unique situation.

Insurance products and annuities are guaranteed by the insurance companies themselves. The safety of these accounts is dependent on the claims paying ability of the insurance companies.

<u>Protect Your Retirement Nest Egg</u>

INTRODUCTION

R.I.P. – Retire in Peace

Most of the time when you see R.I.P. you think of rest in peace on someone's tombstone. However, there are seven immediate steps in 2015 that you must take so that you can truly retire in peace. In this book I will show you critical steps that you must take to protect yourself from losing your retirement nest egg. One of my favorite sayings is…

Simple Retirement equals Simple Life.

There is a motivation that drives me behind what I do, and it was a dear friend of mine, who I will call "Ruth" who was 74 years old. Ruth loaned her 40-year old son her car. He was involved in an accident and someone was killed. The judge ruled a few years later that if that person had lived, their life would have been worth $10 million. Ruth had a $1.2 million IRA retirement account. She lost it, she lost all of her assets. She lost everything she owned, and ultimately ended up homeless because of loaning her son her car that was in her name.

This is just one example of the motivation behind me writing this book, Retire In Peace. Knowing that you have peace of mind and that your retirement is safe and secure. It's that simple - and in the pages to follow I'm going to show you what those simple steps are and how to do it. I use the "Triple S" method: Simple, Safe, and Secure. I will make each step very simple for you, show you how to stay safe, and how to be secure, so that you do not lose your retirement nest egg due to stock market loss, due to the nursing home taking your money away from you, or due to lawsuit-happy attorneys taking your money away from you.

CHAPTER 1

Protect Your Retirement Nest Egg From Stock Market Loss

The first step that I tell all of my client to take so you can retire in peace is to protect your nest egg from the stock market declining and taking it away from you. Wall Street calls this a bearish market, or a bear market. A bear market means that if the market declines, it goes south, and loses money. I have a client in my practice that lost over $1.2 million just due to market loss.

It is critical that the first thing you need to do to protect yourself so that you can retire in peace is make a simple step toward moving your money away from the stock market. I do not mean I am 100% anti-stock market. I am more about being properly allocated with proper amount of risk.

One strategy I like to use is the 100 strategy. It goes something like this: Take the number 100 minus your age. Let's assume you are age 70, or age 75. You take 100 minus 70 equals 30. Or, 100 minus 75 equals 25. That number, 30 or 25, whatever your number is, is the number that you put a percentage sign after, and that is the percentage amount you want to have at risk. So only 25% of your total nest egg should be invested in the stock market. We call that the Rule of 100, or the 100 Rule. If your number is 30, then it simply means 30% of your retirement nest egg is all that needs to be exposed in the stock market.

As Americans, we sometimes forget how bad the stock market can treat us. It is true that sometimes the stock market can treat us very good. For example, if you would have bought

Coca-Cola stock when it very first came out, you would now be a multi-billionaire. I am not anti-stock market, I am just anti-one hundred percent risking everything you have worked your life for in the stock market. Safeguard yourself with a percentage of your retirement being in safety, away from the stock market, so that the stock market does not take it from you. For example, take an IRA, a 401K, or a joint owned account. Suppose it is 100% in the market, and let's assume something tragic happens. We go to war with the Ukraine against Russia. We get involved in a World War III. Anything can happen to make the stock market decline you could lose possibly 50% of your nest egg. Currently the stock market is at an all-time high. I always say it like this: Men, we need to learn from our wives. My wife will drive one hour to the mall just to save money when a 50% sale happens.

The whole idea in the stock market is to buy low, sell high. The Dow topped over 18,000 points in February, 2015. That is an all-time record high. So now would be the time to make a transition and move your money from 100% risk to safety and take some profits off the table. If you're 70, I would recommend to move 70% of your money to safety and then leave the other

30% in the market. By doing this, you are protecting your nest egg from the "bear" of Wall Street taking it away from you. Folks, I have seen many, many clients that worked their entire life and lose their nest egg just due to market loss, because they have too much of it at risk. Their portfolio was 100% invested in the stock market, and they lost everything they had saved for retirement. And it is a tragic situation. Therefore, protect your hard-earned assets from the stock market, from the bear taking it away from you, and instead have the proper amount of diversification in your portfolio.

CHAPTER 2

Protect your Retirement Nest Egg From Nursing Home or Long Term Care

In this chapter, I will talk about how to protect your assets, your estate, your IRA, your nest egg, from the nursing home, or the cost of long-term care taking it away from you.

To put it very simple as we age there is the possibility of being put into the nursing home. Take example in the case of a health issue such as a stroke, heart attack, or cancer. Sometimes it can be an automobile accident. We just simply do not know what the future may hold; it could just be old age. We get too old and have to go into a nursing home. But if you private pay in the Nursing Home, that can quickly eat away at a profitable nest egg. What we as financial advisors recommend is to work with a good Estate Attorney and put all of your assets into an Irrevocable Trust or Catastrophic Illness Trust.

Please understand that I am not an attorney. I do not give legal advice. I do work with a network of attorneys, estate planning attorneys, and I do the financial part by moving the financial assets, be it mutual funds, annuities, life insurance, or whatever financial tool that I need to move into that trust. I work with the attorneys and serve as the financial advisor to move the financial assets into that trust.

It is important to note that an Irrevocable Trust has a five-year look back window. Once you move all of your assets into that trust, you have to wait five years before it is safe from the nursing home. If you are 70, that would mean at age 75, that five-year look back would be behind you. In other states that may vary, but in

Tennessee there is a five-year look back window. If you're 70 years old, then after you turn 75 and you get that five years behind you, then the nursing home cannot take your assets away from you and force you to spin down.

So step two is: Move all of your assets into an Irrevocable Trust so that the nursing home cannot take your hard-earned money, your farm, house, art, jewelry, guns, cars, tractors, or anything that you've worked hard for, and that you've built your entire life to have. It is much smarter to pass it on to your children and your grandchildren than to let a nursing home take it away from you. The way you do that is to put it in an Irrevocable trust and wait 5 years.

CHAPTER 3

Protect Your Retirement Nest Egg From Lawsuits and Judgements

Another important step to take to protect your nest egg, your IRA, your 401K, your CD's, your checking account, or your money market account is to protect yourself from lawsuits and judgements. Anything that you have invested your money in or that you would call your retirement nest egg, even your house or farm, you want to protect. I stated earlier in the introduction of my book about a client of mine, before she became a client of mine, she had loaned her car to her son that was down on his luck, out of a job, and he was involved in an accident that took a person's life. Years down the road, the judge ruled that person, if they would have lived, would have been worth $10 million over their lifetime, because that person was a child that had tragically lost their life. The courts forced her to sell her home and farm, surrender her 1.2 million retirement account, cash in her CD money, everything she had and she was homeless and broke and still owed 7.8 million to fulfill the judgement.

Once again, protect your nest egg from lawsuits and judgements. Today in the world we live in, before we lay our head on a pillow tonight to go to sleep there will be a minimum of three to four TV commercials, or radio commercials, that will simply say, "In a wreck, need a check, call me." Or, "If you get hit by a big truck, call me." "If you take testosterone shots and had a heart attack, call me." Just about every time you're watching the news, or you're reading the newspaper, or you're listening to the news on the radio, there will be advertisements for attorneys just looking to sue somebody that has assets. And it never fails, as many seminars as I do, and as many times as I'm on the radio and listeners call in and talk to me, it never fails that there are very few people that have Irrevocable Trusts, and very few people that have any kind of trust.

Protect your cash, protect your home, protect your automobiles, protect your CD's, protect everything that you have by putting it in an Irrevocable Trust. It becomes lawsuit-proof. There is no creditor, there is no attorney, there is no nursing home that can attach to an Irrevocable Trust.

Some of you reading this book may remember O.J. Simpson. He was convicted in Civil Court for the murder of his wife Nicole Brown Simpson and her boyfriend. In criminal court he was found not guilty and was dismissed, and was not charged for criminal murder. However, on the civil side he was convicted. A $38 million dollar judgment is how much the Brown family was awarded against O.J. Simpson.

The interesting point here is he had all of his IRA money, and all of his assets in an Irrevocable Trust, therefore the Brown family could not attach the judgment to that Irrevocable

Trust. They have collected nothing from the $38 million dollar judgment. Irrevocable Trusts are judgment proof, lawsuit proof, nursing home proof, and they are creditor-proof. Get started today and move all your assets, get it away from lawsuits happy attorneys where they cannot take it away from you with frivolous judgements.

CHAPTER 4

Protect Your Retirement Nest Egg From Passing Through Probate

The next step you want to take is, to avoid probate and unnecessary taxes from taking away your retirement. In order to retire in peace, you want to avoid the probate process. You want to avoid unnecessary taxes being levied against your retirement. One of the best ways to simplify retirement, and therefore simplify your life, is to be sure everything is set up to avoid probate. The only fail-proof way to avoid probate and unnecessary taxes is a good, fully-funded Revocable Living Trust. There are two types of trusts. You have been hearing me talk about the Irrevocable Trust, but there is also a Revocable Living Trust. Once again please understand, I am not giving you legal advice, I am not licensed to do that. I am not an attorney, however I do work with a network of attorneys, and I have been involved in many trusts and moving financial assets into those trusts.

Over 18 trillion dollars will change hands as this generation passes their estates to their heirs. This is referred to as the 18 trillion dollar secret, because the IRS wants to capture as much of it as possible in inheritance taxes. This transfer will take place through the probate process. The largest percentage of impact from the cost of probate is on estates of $1 million or less. Typically probate fees are six to ten percent. While $6,000 and $100,000 may not seem like a large amount, the impact could be catastrophic, because probate fees are calculated on the gross size of your estate, not your net estate. Why the gross size? Because the court has to make sure that your debts, probate, and attorney fees are paid before it can pay your assets to your heirs. Therefore the fees are calculated on your entire estate, including your debts.

It is important that you understand only having a "Will", will take you through probate. In order to retire in peace, and simplify your retirement, which will simplify your life, the next step you need to take in avoiding probate and unnecessary taxes is to have a fully-funded Revocable Living Trust. With a Revocable Living Trust, you will avoid probate. An easy way to remember this is if all you have is a "Will" you "will" go through probate. The attorneys will eat away at it, six to ten percent of your estate will be their fees. It could take up to one or two years for the distribution, and there will be public disclosure of your assets, debts, and heirs. The maximum negative emotional impact on your family will be horrible. The court will appoint, in some cases, if you have minor children, a guardianship or conservatorship over your estate if all you have is a Will. The maximum estate taxes will be charged. And, a Will is very easily contested.

Once again, to retire in peace, just simply move your nest egg into a Revocable Living Trust. There is no court control. There are no probate fees. There is no chance of a conservatorship being appointed, or a guardian if you have minor children. You determine who the conservator is, you determine who the guardian is to raise your minor children,. There is no hassle and delay. It is totally, 100 percent private and family controlled. There are no unnecessary expenses, no unnecessary taxes, and it even contains a no-contest clause.

Be sure you simplify your retirement, and your life, and retire in peace. Be sure that you avoid the probate process and any unnecessary taxes.

CHAPTER 5

Protect Your Retirement Nest Egg by Choosing The Correct Trust

In order to simplify your retirement, and your life, so you can Retire in Peace, you want to make sure you choose the correct trust. Just go to Google and type in the word "trust." There are around 19,000 trusts. It can be very confusing.

The network of attorneys I work with are through a company called The Estate Plan. They specialize in Ir-revocable and Revocable Living Trusts.

A book I highly recommend is called *The Living Trust* by Henry W. Abts, III. It is the fail-proof way to pass along your estate to your heirs, without courts getting involved, or without going through the probate system.

The Estate Plan has been around for more than 28 years. They have more than 1,000 attorneys. Not all living trusts are created equal. The biggest differences in the 19,000 trusts out there, and the reason that I use The Estate Plan is because it's approved in all 50 states. They have

28 years of history behind them, and they are very good at what they do. They are the best in the Nation !

There are five key differences in The Estate Plan Trust that I want to point out to you that makes them the best in the nation.

Number one: There are 222 must-have provisions in an estate Living Trust and The Estate Plan knows what they are.

Number two: There are state-specific ancillary documents, and The Estate Plan is very familiar with those for not only the State of Tennessee but every state in the country.

Number three: They custom-draft the trust to fit your needs and incorporate a Will, Living Will, Dual Power of Attorney, Medical Power of Attorney, etc.

Number four: As I mentioned earlier, they have developed these trusts over 28 years, and several times these trusts have been challenged in court, and not one single time has The Estate Plan Trust lost nor have the courts ever been able to pierce The Estate Plan trust.

Number five: It is designed to cover every potential contingency. The documents with The Estate Plan have been reviewed and evaluated by many experts over the past 28 years, and it is just simply an ironclad Living Revocable Living Trust that is done properly, it is done accurately, and it has withstood the test of time. Take the next step and be sure that it is the right, correct, proper trust, and that an attorney just hasn't went out on Google and grabbed any old Google trust and stuck you in it. Ask your attorney or financial advisor if they use The Estate Plan.

Chapter 6

Protect Your Retirement Nest Egg

by Choosing the Correct Advisor

Choose the correct advisor. Make absolutely sure the advisor that you are talking with is FINRA/SIPC approved, that they are security licensed. There are a lot of life insurance-only salespeople running around claiming to be financial advisors. All that a life insurance sales person can write you is a life insurance product or an annuity. There is nothing wrong with life insurance products, and there is nothing wrong with annuities, but it takes a licensed advisor to determine if an annuity or life insurance product is the investment vehicle needed for you and your financial plan. Therefore, if they only carry a life insurance license, they are not properly qualified to diagnose your financial situation. Legally and by law they cannot give you advice about your mutual funds or anything tied to the stock market. This would include your 401K or IRA.

Make sure that you choose the correct investment advisor, or financial advisor, whichever term you want to use.   Just be absolutely sure that they are securities licensed, FINRA/SIPC approved, security licensed advisors. This way they are qualified to talk with you about your retirement.   If you are not careful, some life insurance salesman will try to give you financial advice and stick you in an annuity or a life insurance product that may or may not be "fiducially" speaking what is best for you, because that is all they can write, and they cannot give you financial advice.

I would like to give you two things that every retiree should do when choosing an Investment Advisor.

First, you should always get a second opinion. This will help you retire in peace. This will help you simplify your retirement, simplify your life. Let's be honest here. If you went to the doctor tomorrow and were diagnosed with cancer, you would go get a second opinion. So even if you currently have a financial advisor and they are not life insurance only-licensed, but they are a true financial advisor, you should still get a second opinion from a FINRA, securities licensed, SIPC approved financial advisor, just for a second set of eyes.

The second thing you want to do is to make sure that you know what questions to ask that financial advisor. It always surprises me when people go to an advisor's office, they will just take whatever the advisor says, and they will never ask a question. Know what questions to ask the advisor. It is like choosing a doctor. I am surprised that nobody asks their doctor what grades they made in medical school but they let that doctor do surgery on them. Wouldn't it make sense to ask questions ?

What do you call a person who graduated last in their class, and passed with a D, on their medical exam during medical school? You call that person a doctor. Nobody ever asks their doctor what was your grade on your medical exam, what was your ranking in your class of students. Would it make you uneasy to know that this doctor is about to perform open heart surgery on you, or cut out a cancerous tumor, but yet he or she finished last in their class and barely made a D just to pass, to get by? But yet they are getting ready to open you up and do open heart surgery or cut a tumor out, and you never slowed down long enough to ask them. Here are a few important questions to ask your financial advisor:

1. What grade did you make on your final exam or did you make a D to barely pass ?

2. Where is your personal money invested in, the market or secure investments ?

3. Are you life insurance licensed-only, or are you securities licensed ? Are you a FINRA/SIPC approved securities advisor? Are you fiducially responsible for me, not just suitability? Any securities licensed FINRA/SIPC approved advisor is fiduciary

responsible to do the best thing for you according to the law.

Chapter 7

Protect Your Retirement Nest Egg by Staying Committed To The Plan

Once you have addressed the other six steps and are finally comfortable with the advisor you have chosen, the final step is to stick with the plan you and your advisor have mapped out. Stay committed. Allow the plan time to work. Wait on it to happen. Don't let your neighbor next door convince you that they heard about a new company that's getting ready to do an IPO, which is Initial Placement Offering, and you can buy in at 50 cents and it's going to go to

$300 a share, and so you abort the plan, you pull all of your money out, and you stick it in this new company that's doing an Initial Placement Offer. Don't do that !!! Once you have chosen an approved advisor, once you've got a plan, stick to the plan, stick to the process, and trust the process.

If you will apply the seven steps that I've shown you in this book, you will retire in peace. You will have a simple retirement, which will produce a simple stress free life.

It takes time to plan. You spend time planning a family vacation so take the same time to plan your retirement, you will be glad you did so you can truly Retire In Peace.